T0121994

Smelling My Own Coffee

Sixty-Five Moments of Thought

Poetry and Prose

CAROL SAMUELS

iUniverse, Inc.
New York   Bloomington

Smelling My Own Coffee
Sixty-Five Moments of Thought

iUniverse books may be ordered through booksellers or by contacting:

iUniverse
1663 Liberty Drive
Bloomington, IN 47403
www.iuniverse.com
1-800-Authors (1-800-288-4677)

ISBN: 978-1-4502-6515-7 (sc)
ISBN: 978-1-4502-6514-0 (ebook)
ISBN: 978-1-4502-6513-3 (dj)

Printed in the United States of America

iUniverse rev. date: 11/22/2010

Table of Contents

INTRODUCTION

SMELLING MY OWN COFFEE: 64 moments of thought is a book of answers that touch hopefully on every segment of life. Throughout this book the use of language, its' importance and the impact of words verbal and non-verbal is expressed. I tried to impart secret feelings, lack of feelings, universal feelings, feelings of love, hate, loss, quiet encouragement and faith. Especially important is the need to feel what, when, where, how and just because. The purpose of the book is to answer or give meaning to all the words in the glossary by way of various selections of poems, statements, thoughts, and vignettes that address the virtues, principles, and very substances of life.

DEDICATION

I GIVE SPECIAL THANKS TO MY IMMEDIATE AND EXTENDED FAMILY WHOSE LIFE EXPIERENCES CREATED MY POSITIVE WORLD.

MAY THE MOST HIGH BLESS THEM ALL WITH GOOD AND VERY GOOD.
MAY NOTHING STEAL THEIR HAPPINESS, DECREASE THEIR FAITH, BLOCK THEIR BLESSINGS, CHANGE THEIR VALUES, BIND THEIR LOVE, INTERFERE WITH THEIR SUCCESS OR LIMIT THEIR PROSPERITY

DEDICATED TO MY LOVING PARENTS, MILDRED AND GEORGE, BROTHERS GEORGE AND JAMES, AND CHILDREN MONIFA, KONATA, NATAKI, BRITTANY, MARCUS, DEAN AND DEAR HUSBAND ROBERT.
MAY THEY ALWAYS HAVE PERFECT HEALTH OF BODY AND MIND
PEACE, HARMONY, SUCCESS AND PROSPERSITY.

IN MEMORY OF AUNT HILDA WHO WATCHES OVER ME...........

1. WORDS

Words written without meaning

Words uttered without thoughts

Words heard without understanding

Words spoken without feeling

Words used as tools

Words used as weapons

Words used as manipulators

And a lot of times it's even

The absence of words that

Causes the abuse of words

With this in mind how should

I speak to thee

Should I write love letters

To melt your heart

Should I cuss and stamp to

Shock and upset you

Should I tease and threaten you

To scare and frighten you

Should I tell you my feelings

Only to have them misconstrued

Twisted around and used against me

There should be a law against

Words not used to comfort

There should be a law against

Words not used as lullabies

There should be a law against

Words not used to bring joy

..............in fact

There should be no language

With words other than those

Needed to express

        Sincere

           Love and caring

2. MELT DOWN ......

I wake each morning wandering

If the world is still intact

Turn the light on wondering if

We have had a blackout.....

And since this movie China syndrome

Wandering if we are having a meltdown....

Then with the thoughts of death,

The anxiety heightens and I wonder...

Why you can't treat me better

In this life.....Why you can't tell me

You love me... Why you can't tell me

I'm beautiful... Why you can't tell me

I'm smart...Why you can't say

You miss me all day... Why can't you say

You work every day so you can give me

The moon..

Food doesn't have taste until

I cook it and put it on your plate...

Words don't have sound until

I say them...clothes don't have color

Until I wear them...put me on a pedestal

And call me princess... that is the way

I want to be treated ...that's what I want

To hear...

In fact I have come to the

Conclusion all I want you to do is

Lie to me...lie to me and make me sing and

Dance...lie to me and make my head spin...

Lie to me and make me jump up and down

Or better yet don't lie to me!!!!....

Try saying I'm not beautiful....

I'm not smart...I'm not rich and you

Can't buy me the moon...and you don't

Know anything about a pedestal...

Say my cooking isn't great...my

Sewing is lousy...and my cleaning is

Mediocre...but!!!! , even with that

Against me you can't fight loving me!!!

Now lord I don't know if the earth is

Ready .... but behind a few words like that

Wow!!! It would be just a matter of a

Count down ...before my personal

Melt down!!!!!!

3. FRIENDSHIP LOVE

Hello or should I say hello...

Hello and how are you is the

Usual and yet it's not just right...

After all most people using hello

And how are you just use it as

A phrase not as greetings and

Salutations ...but as greetings and

Hallucinations...yes hallucinations...

Yes the greeting is there but....

Your answer to how are you makes

Little or no difference,

It's like saying hell-o ...hell did I have to see you,

And Oh well since I did ...not hel-lo

God bless you and I'm glad I have

a chance to greet you....

But I do want to say this...

I want to say hello and how are you...

Because the more I think of you

The more I think of you.

So don't tell me how you are...

I want to see how you are...

I want to see by the way

you walk, whether each step is firm...

Whether each step follows the previous

Like a note in a harmony

Or should I say does the melody of your footsteps ride

easy on my ears.... let me look at you,

at your eyes are they shallow pools

of heartache wanting to cry out,

Are they bloodshot with confusion?

No don't tell me how you are, ...

Let me feel you, touch you, see if your

head is hot with fever, if you're neck

cold with tension, if your hands are

clammy with nervousness or hard with

pent-up hostility,

Let me feel your shoulders do they become rigid to my

touch...but most of all ...let me embrace

you just for a second...

It's long enough

to know if all is well...

How would you look if I said I love you...

Would you look at me the way you did

when you saw me with someone else...

Hating yet hurt.... speechless yet screaming

obscenities ...

Staring with eyes that stabbed...

I could say that I understood but would it

be true and was it fair for you to condemn...

But then have I been fair with you.

Have I not put you on a pedestal and loved and

worshipped you and expected you to live

in the narrow guidelines that are in my mind,

Narrow because they didn't include all

things or weren't prepared for all things,

Narrow because if you sometimes deviated

from what I thought should be your natural

course...

I was shaken, upset, maddened.......

Because I would feel it was beneath you...

Had I judged you too highly?

I no!!! never....

But aren't we all guilty of being too stagnant

I with your loved ones...I ask how would you

feel if I said I love you, ...

A love so sweet and innocent and gentle...

like a warm breeze engulfing you, protecting you, smoothing and

comforting you.... a spiritual love in my soul,

in my mind, in my body....

What if I said my heart beats for you, but that wouldn't be true

My heart beats for me in my body...this is deeper,

This is in my soul and my mind.... time can't erase

it or weaken it,.... and what would you say if I said

I love you... and I don't have to see you to love you,

I have seen you ... I don't have to speak to you,

to love you, I have spoken to you,.... I don't have to

touch you to love you, I have touched you...

Then would you ask yourself .....then why would

I say I love you if not to be with you.....

Could it be to let you know that in your moments of

loneliness... you're not alone...in your moments

of hopelessness all is not bleak,

To let you know when you are down ..

There is someone to help you up...when you are sad I'd like to make

you happy...I will always have a shoulder for

you to lean on, an open ear to listen and a

hand stretched out ... I'm not your lover....

But I will always love you ....

I am your friend ...if you need me just call

I'll have time for you because I'll make time for

you,.... friend........

4.   ESCAPADE

I said 29...he thought 40.....

I felt 50... he acted 35.........

It was all wrong.....

And yet...such a delight

I was tall ...he was short

We were both the same

height....

Looking in his eyes

Gave me such a

wonderful fright.....

5.   ROSE COLORED GLASSES

How many times need I say I love you,

How many times need I shed the same

tears and how many times will you

wipe them away and not even know I cried

...or smile and nod without hearing a word

...how many times will my screams be muffled

by the many other problems of the day....

No you can't see my tears in the rain

No you can't hear my screams in my laughter

No you can't judge my hunger by the plate

before me

No you can't feel the pain that dwells

deep within me...

Will an aspirin here,.. a tissue there....

Maybe a joke now... food and water.....

Then... solve mine and the woes of the

world...maybe yes but how can I say???

I'm afraid to think the thoughts that

would ask the questions that could...

Would give me the reasons why.... or

maybe it is not the reasons why but

how...how do I find my way back through

the woods...in from the rain...out of the

darkness....

Yes I walked the plains and I know there

is no shelter...yes I experienced the calm

Before the storm...yes I heard that light

can be so blinding.... but there is a way a passage,

It is not north...it is not south...it is not west

...it is not east...we all know that it is not up...

Since we know not which direction that is....

So maybe we'll just settle down....

Yes I shall go jogging, what better time

To set my pace after all my stage is set

And as long as I am to be this character

Then I should perform...could life be more

than a performance.....

Could love be more than a show...do we not take cue from the

next actor and then act our part until

we're interrupted by the next fool to perform.....

Questions.... questions.... to be answered by

questions with questions which give way to more questions...

No let's not give answers for that may end my

Depression...no let's not give answers for it

Would kill my frustrations...no let's not give

answers for it would dry my eyes... no let's not

give answers for it would heal my wounds....

No let's not give answers for it will fulfill

my hunger...

Let's just reach for the rose colored glasses....

Yes the show must go on.....you're playing your

part oblivious to the rest of the world.... but

for some strange reason... every so often you

look, no you stare and there's sympathy...no.

there's empathy.... no there is tenderness.... no

there's sadness.... could you be seeing me....

my pain... my tears.... my shattered dreams....

Or could

     You just

       Be looking

         Over your

           Rose colored glasses

And seeing the real you that I mirror.........

6.   UP....DOWN.....AROUND....

UP....DOWN.....AROUND....

I HEARD THE WORD UP

AND I LOOKED UP...

I HEARD THE WORD DOWN

AND I LOOKED DOWN.....

I HEARD THE WORD LOVE

AND I LOOKED ALL AROUND

     ..... AROUND

       ....AROUND

..........AROUND

7.   EGO TRIPPING

He asked me did I miss him

and I said yes

He asked me did I need him

and I said yes

He asked me did I love him

and I said yes

He asked did I want him

and I said no....

No I don't want you

if you have to ask do I miss

you...

No I don't want you

If you have to ask do I need

you

No I don't want you

If you have to ask do I love

you

You can see by my eyes that

I love you...

You can feel by my touch that

I need you.....

You can tell from my embrace

that I miss you...

No I don't want you 'cause your

asking tells me this is not love

You're in...

it is an ego trip you are on

You may think that you love me

but you don't

You may think that you're infatuated

with me, but ...you're not

No I don't want you.......

You might even miss my missing you

when I'm gone....

You might need my needing you

when I'm gone

You might even hate my loving you

when I'm gone 'cause the ego be's that

way...

The ego wants,

The ego needs,

The ego misses

but the ego doesn't give....

The ego doesn't love.....

So no I don't want you......

8.   LOVE

Love is merely a four lettered word

That can't be measured

...........can't be weighed...

.........can't be used

...can't be abused

...can't be broken

..... can't be crushed

...can't be rushed

..can't be seen

Can't be smelled

Can't be tasted

Can't be wasted

Can't be touched

Can't be felt

Can't be eatened

Can't be drunk.

Can't be defined ....and

yet.... it's been proven to......

Make the sick, well

Make the small, grow

Make the hungry, full

 Make the blind, see

Make the crippled, walk

Make the deaf, hear

Make the dumb, talk

Make the bad, good

Make the weak, strong

Make the old, young

and

      make

          the

          heart

            beat.!!!!!!!!

9.   NO THOUGHT

She needed to think a thought an

idea, a preponderance, a mental image

but none came

she felt a forcing, a pushing,

a pulling, maybe just a yearning....

her mind was blank, bleak, dead

No this was not death

death has a way of making your

life pass before you.... not this

lost muddy weird whirlpool of

nothingness

Or had the mind just have taken

off and left for the day, for the

moment, forever.... without giving

that last run back, that final

replay that last fling of repentance

If she could just think about

what to think about or maybe this

was what her mind was escaping....

Her constant mental chaos, her mental
jungle, her mental wars of smaller
mental battles fighting for
individual attentions.... no...
lets hope not, for her last thoughts
were too many, about too many things
of no importance

Importance.... priorities..... concrete
realities...wow, now that's some heavy
powerful thought words right there,
those kinds of idea words could lead
lead you straight to philosophy, 'round
ideology, through theology and right up
beside intellectuality......

No we can be sure her mind had never
tangled with any thoughts, words,
ideas, visions or dreams that would
ever make her think thoughts along
those lines or surely we would
understand why her mind was blank,
blown, shot, or dead...

At long last have we figured her out,

could her thoughts of nothingness,

of beauty, of monsters, of television,

of fantasies unbiased lead her down

this road...could it be she finally has

thought the last nothing thought,

leaving her with nothing left to

think about... could she have thought

all the nothing thoughts worth

and unworth thinking about.........

10. TIME'S A WASTING

You ponder, wonder, think,

and thought about it

But...... time's a wasting

Yes I should, now that I have considered

this and that

wait, no ...I shouldn't when I

study that and the other

but on the other hand I could

reconsider......

But..... time's a wasting

No, naw, maybe not

Yes, if only ... sure...

A definite maybe...

If and but.....

But........ time's a wasting

Wait let me rest, regroup, think,

Meditate on this then.......

I shall get down to business

And I shan't lose a minute....

But........ time's a wasting.

11. LANGUAGE SWITCH

I say sit and they're on their feet

I say quiet and conversation flourishes

I say sleep and they become wide awake

I say eat and their appetite leaves

So what is a mother to do

Alas...I have got it...

I have been speaking English when

the language they understand is

children...

So, now I have switched languages

I say nicely stand over there

You can be sure they will go and sit

I ask who is responsible for this or

that and immediately a hush comes

over the room

I say go to your room and study

and everyone goes straight to sleep

I say I am not cooking and everyone

decides they want to eat....

There is only one problem

At what age do I switch

back to English..........

12.   LOVE FROM WHERE

You listen and wonder from what

direction does love come ....from

where does love evolve, or does it

bloom like a flower from a seed

planted in the mind or heart,

fertilized with tears, and using

rays of joy as sunlight,

Or maybe it is like a vitamin processed like food,

once you have eatened the thoughts

of another,   if the body can handle it,

it is turned to nourishment and adds

to the strength and fiber of the body,

to the life and glow of the body......

or is it your repentance...

your emotional succumbance,...your

lesson in humbleness ... your equilibrium

which puts you in balance and in touch

with the ultimate apex, yet making you

acknowledge that the lost of it would

be like being pushed into a bottomless pit.

Oh lord does it come from you as a gift

or is it sent from the devil as a torment,

as delicious as the forbidden fruit.....

is it sweet as candy ...captivating and

suffocating as quicksand......

Does it overwhelm you like a tornado

sucking you in and throwing you around,

yet never turning you loose...

Could it be like a warm breeze in the

spring twilight, could it be the beauty

of the setting sun on the horizon,

Could it be the light feminine. scent

of jasmine blowing in the air, or the macho

scent of water after a hard rain on the

fresh cut grass...

Or can it be simply be

summed up as chemistry......

like the amount of acid in your saliva

or the amount of salt in your tears

and perspiration,

Or does it gallop in from the east like a

horse of fiery.......

bucking and snorting and kicking

wildly at its peak and then

slowly

leveling

      off

      to a quiet

self contained confidently

satisfying calm contentment,

that surrounds you much like

sound

     sleep

         engulfs

            a baby........

.

13.   ALL IN A SPIN

Up down turnaround he got

     himself a pocket of rocks

Up down turnaround he got

     himself a little wife

Up down turnaround he got

     himself a big house

Up down turnaround he got

     himself two kids

Up down turn around in and out

     and all about town

Up down turnaround he got

     himself a divorce now..........

14. YELLOW ROSE

She stood cold, oh so cold in this
damp and cold weather, it had
come so suddenly so as to firmly
mark the end of the summer and
announce winter even before
the fall.... the wind seemed not
to blow but to bite into her
with its coldness.... and where
was the sun, the warm rays of
the sun or was it just too cold
even for it......

Cold..... but she stood stiff and
straight against the cold and
wind bracing herself as if it
would pass her unnoticed........
She stood rigid as if frozen
Solid, the lightest fall would
surely shatter her into a
million pieces........
Would she succumb?

Could she relax and let this pierce her....

and let her life and beauty be drained from

her until the spring.... when the

ground and weather would once

again welcome this yellow rose.

15. JUST OUT HAVING A DRINK

Yeah Sam play it again

Yeah Sam play it again

Play that down home funky blues

Play that song about that no good man

Play that song about that no count woman

Yeah Sam play it again

So I can go home and beat my

woman for things you say she

did ...and I can fantasize

about the things you say I did

Yeah Sam play that down

home funky blues..........

So I can become part of the world

we are all supposed to come from

and.........

Yeah Sam let me have one more

drink...and

Yeah Sam play that

down home funky blues...

16. WHEN SHE DIED ALL THEY SAID WAS SHE WAS A HOOKER

She was a hooker

but was not that her right

She was a hooker

cause her body was such a lovely sight

She was a hooker

and she brought many men delight

She was a hooker

cause she had her own idea of wrong and right

Hooking was her game

Hooking brought her fame

Hooking was the specialty of this dame

but for you all left behind

with that she was a hooker line

I have found out she was not

without her sadness

I have found out she was not

without her pain

I have found out she was not

without her needs

I have found out she was not

without her wants and loneliness

as she moved right along

But for you all left behind with

that she was a hooker line

You know you cannot figure her

success

You know you cannot measure her

happiness

You know you cannot sense her

agonies

But for you all left behind with

that she was a hooker line

Hooker she was whether wrong

or right

Hooker she was maybe not to her

delight

Hooker she was but a mother's

babe too

Hooker she was but a sister,

wife, mother, aunt, niece, cousin

and someone's friend too

Hooker she was...but should this

have wiped out at any hour...

what was her right to life...?

17.   .... AND SHE WAS GIVEN SENILITY

She was told she was tired

She was told she was sad

She was told she was unhappy

And depressed

She was told she was alone

She was told she was bored

She was told she was sick

Inside she wanted to be full of

Fun

Inside she wanted to be full of

Pep

Inside she wanted to be full of

Adventure and rearing to go

But there was nowhere to go

Fore unfortunately she was

Classified as old and she

Knew that ....that meant

She was sick

She was bored

She was alone

She was depressed

She was unhappy

She was sad

She was tired ...and

All these classifications

And limitations on her

mind was making her

S e n i l e...

18. MOVING FAST GOING NOWHERE

WHEN WE ARE YOUNG WE MOVE FASTER

THEN TIME

WHEN WE ARE OLD TIME MOVES FASTER

THEN US

THEN TOGETHER WE BOTH COME TO A

STAND STILL GOING NO WHERE

19.   IN THE VERY END ....NO STRINGS ATTACHED

From the very beginning

I have held your hand

Given you firm hugs

Wiped your tears

Listened to your woes

Smiled at your jokes

Shared your anger

Stroked your ego

Boosted your self-esteem

Tickled your fancy

Soothed your pain

Rocked you like a babe

And quieted your fears

With no strings attached...

With no strings attached

I ask only that you hold my

Hand in the very end

However if you can't be there

For me in the very end......

My knowing that you will

Have had and cherished

These simple memories....

Will comfort me and continue

Our everlasting love

With no strings attached

20.   SILENCE

Listen to the silence

It can be heralding

Listen to the silence

It can be deafening

Listen to the silence

It can be overwhelming

Listen, listen, listen

To the silence......

For so much is said in

silence

For so much is heard in

silence

The right answers come

boldly...

      In

            the

                silence.........

21. IN MY SOLITUDE

In my solitude, in my quiet,

I retreat from the world

I smile at my thoughts

Laugh at my own jokes

Cry at my hidden hurts

I listen to my inner voice

which gives both hindsight

and foresight.....

I sing to the lyrics and

dance to the melodies

of rhythm and blues

I ponder wealth issues

I ponder health issues

I ponder political issues

I ponder religious issues

I mentally design bathrooms

and bedrooms

Plan menus and decorate

cakes

In my solitude I come alive

and live... in my solitude...

22.   DIVINE ORDER

I do not want to know how

the world runs

I just know how I run and go

Divine substance is my supply

My run and go

I do not need to see

Jane run, spot go, and Sally stop

I just know that Divine substance

is my supply

My run and go until I stop

and Divine substance will see me

through

Grace let everything

else run in Divine Order

until it is all time to

Divinely stop.............

23. THINGS TO DO ALONG THE WAY

Life is a long road to travel

with few sign post

So along the way....

do unto others as you wish

them to do unto you

See life as good and it will be

good to you

Be good to yourself and people

close to you

They in turn will be good to

you along the way......

Treat everyone like you want to

be treated with respect and

caring and they will treat you

with respect and caring

along the way.....

Relax, take life one day at a

time and have a good time

We all have to learn how

to care for and love each other

It takes work to be good to

each other...but it pays well

Make love not war, you will

live longer and happier and

win more battles with less scars

Learn to give compliments and

accept compliments....

Give thanks for the little things

along the way....

while you learn to forgive

yourself and all others for

all things past, present and

future........ these are just

things to do along the way!

24.   SCREAMING SILENTLY

I sit for hours thinking of you

wondering if I knew you in some

pass life

watching you and wanting to be

around you.... loving your spirit and

cherishing your soul.....

I want to sit and talk to you

or just sit near you watching

silently, waiting for you to say

something, and then give that

satirical smile followed by a

blink of those dancing sadistic

eyes, I watch as you move and

converse...objectively and cold

with such great command and control.

I cannot but wonder if someone has

hurt you along the way. this only

more emphasizes my need to touch

and caress you each time upon meeting

and leaving you. I come to visit you

only to find you are out. ..this does not

alarm me, for I smile, and hope

this means you are out somewhere

enjoying yourself and wonder,

if you indeed have friends,

thus not knowing or noticing

my admiration for you......

I think of you always before I sleep

and upon awaking in the midst of

the night ...I sit often and daydream

about you, when I should be

doing other things...then I can not

condemn myself for I feel the time

well spent.... my love of you have

brought me an abundance of silent

joy and sorrow, screaming silently

to be shared with you..... but though

I yearn to be your object of affection

I exist each day content to

                        scream

                             silently......

25.   IN YOUR SADNESS

I came into your life

to help to make you happy

in your sadness

I came into your life

to help to make you happy

and your smile came.....

in your sadness

I came into your life

to help to make you happy

and your smile came

I leave you now

before you have time to laugh

in your sadness

I came into your life

to help to make you happy

and your smile came

I leave you now before you have

time to laugh

I leave you with a smile

and a deeper sadness comes

26. AND THE MOON REMAINS

When the need was there

I raped the moon

I basked in the moonlight

and smiled.....

taken into its confidence and

questioned it 'til my needs

were satisfied and smiled.......

I raped the moon when the

need was there.....

and the moon remains

unchanged......

27.   HAPPINESS IS ....

Happiness is lollipop sticks

and sticky face pressed on the

mirror,

greasy fingers and mouth full of fried

chicken

mommy I love you and daddy wanting a

backrub

happiness is everything that brings

a little smile or tears of joy

happiness is finding no runs in your

stockings, and money hidden in your

coat pockets, no additional gray hairs

and wrinkle free satin sheets

happiness is sunset and bubble bath

sweet potatoes, dry wine, Nina Simone,

Langston Hughes and Frederick Douglas

happiness is an evening with Malcolm

Betty and three months in Kampala

Happiness is the joy of today....

mixed with the experiences of

yesterday and the plans of

tomorrow

Happiness is not a miracle

nor is life or death

It is just a way of seeing

things through the heart's

eyes........

28.   WHAT DO I KNOW OF LIFE

What do I know of life

I know nothing of life

I know yakwak is the basis

does the sun warm the heart

rain washes the body

love comforts the soul

happiness raises the spirit

but what of you, my dear

do I love thee

there are no stars shining

when I see you

no bells ringing when I listen

to you

no goose pimples from your touch

no breathlessness from anxiety

due to your presence

so I ask again ...what do I know of life

I know nothing of life

honey is sweet

warm breezes are soothing

champagne is tintillating

trees give oxygen and....

the oceans are full of fish

but what of you my dear

I yearn to be near you

yet your presence does not

excite me and...

your absence never alarms me

but I pray for you

       before I pray for me

so I ask again...

what do I know of life

I know nothing of life

is it your lack of mystery that

eludes me.... or you're overwhelming

simplicity that puts me on guard

so what do I know of life

if my suspected love

       perplexes me...........

29.   MOONSHINE

Moonshine shimmering on the

ocean's water

Moonshine sparkling like diamonds

on dew frosting the blue grass

pastures

Moonshine clear, cool, cold, colorless

yet shining in an air of peacefulness

Moonshine mellow almost shyly showing

one side only to those who peer

Moonshine hypnotically almost mockingly

exposing more than less....

Less than more than the night before

30.   RAINBOW

When the rainbows

     the rainbow's

          rainbows

scream... holler...shout ...lightning ...thunder

as the rainbows

     The rainbows

          Rainbow's

     rainbows

scream...holler.... shout...lightning.... thunder

But the rainbow rainbows for

     cupid's arrows of lightning

     struck sun rays

scream...holler...shout...lightning...thunder

31. DAY AND NIGHT

Day and night teaches you

two things..to laugh and cry

laugh when there is hope

and cry when things seem hopeless

for these are lessons often used

in the days and nights of your life..

and we move from hope to hopelessness

Sometimes as quickly as we move from

crying to laughter and very often

As smoothly as day and night

32.   -SUNRISE ..... SUNSET

Let the sun rise on your head

Let the sun set on your back

Let the sun rise on your head

Let the sun set on your back

Rise sun on my head and burn my eyes red

Rise sun and turn my skin black

Rise sun and warm my lazy bones

Set sun on my back let me rest

my weary bones

Set sun and take your rays out

of my eyes

Set sun and cool my tired ass

Let the sun rise on your head

Let the sun set on your back

Let the sun rise on your head

Let the sun set on your back

Rise sun on another day of work

Rise sun and let me get out

here for all it is worth

Rise sun and make these crops

grow tall so I got plenty

to pick and they got plenty

to eat

Rise sun and let my days be long

and numbered

for I know I ain't worth no more

than I am strong

Let the sun rise on my head

cause I know sure as the sun

rise each day

before I want it

it will surely set on my back

and close all my days before

I realize it ....

33. NO LIFE/SUICIDE

They

watch the

body for signs

of life

still

I lay

no one ever

thought me

life

of the

party or show

but still

cold

I lay

as they watch on

for signs

dead

no life

curiously

too much

love

too late

locked up in death

I lay

34. CAROL

I was sent here with a purpose

and that purpose was to put

some harmony in the lives

of the people I come in touch

with in my life time.

I am here only for this purpose

and only for a short amount

of time...I won't stay forever

and I am not here to give harmony

to the whole world...just the

people I come in contact with

in the short amount of time

I am here...

They did not yank

me from my mother's wound

for nothing other than this

one purpose and such they

labeled me C a r o l ...since

my life's purpose is that of a

song... a Carol is soothing

to the heart, is sweetness

to the ears, comforting to

a baby, inspirational to the

spirit and sweet music to

the soul...

As time goes on

I try hard to forefill my

purpose..... in my heart

knowing when I have gone

on to another level...I.

would be happy for a job

well done...

Will I be remembered for

being humane, for being

sentimental or better yet

will I be remembered as I live

traveling incognito as a song

in a body, like a Carol on the

wind.... And may my life be

like dust ...noticed when I

am there... but never missed

after I am gone...

35. REHABILITATION...LEARNING TO WALK AGAIN

It is like being spanked as a child

You brace yourself against the blows

cringe and bite your teeth

with each strike

Finally you scream and cry and

the pain is no longer the point

as your attention is now

held by your own screams

and the process of executing

these screams

And like a child you live through it

and learn to walk again

rehabilitated..........

36. LIFE

God let me live slowly

let not a sun rise and set

determine yet another day

for it goes far too fast

For each day gone should

be a guarantee of another

day yet to be lived...

extend my life until I feel tired

For the joy of life

invigorates me eternally

and my time should surely

not run out

Rejoice I this day and file

it away for me to recapture

as a time to jump back to

and sweetly relive these

moments of joy

For this life lived only

once is definitely not enough

For the sweetness should be

savored with delight of

ecstatic ecstasy..

Let me live and enjoy until my

senses are rubbed raw and

may each sensitivity be

amplified and highly

stimulated by the living of

this life

37. THE LORD SPEAKS

The Lord speaks to me when I

smile while my body screams

with pain...

The Lord speaks to

me when he assures me you

are not my pain, but my inspiration

The lord speaks to me when he

gives me the patience to listen

to you explain to me your problems

yet keeping mine between He and I

The Lord speaks to me when He sees

 me through another days work,

though fussing and tired and in

constant pain while all the time

giving thanks to you for your

compliments of a job well done

He speaks to me each day when

I open my eyes on a brand new

day....

38.   BUT I AM NOT TURNING YOU DOWN

She looked right at him ...and

he asked what she was into

She answered softly.....

classical music, metaphysics,

poetry, and abstract art ...

and for recreation and relaxation

she liked sweet wine and well

done steaks accompanied

with bullshit conversation...

She added she was intimate

with only one man and had

no more under her cap, then

Einstein..... hated fresh cut

flowers - which represented

murder of one of the earth's

prettiest species...

But I am not turning you down

He felt confident and thought he

would take her up on the sweet wine,

well done steaks, and definitely

the bullshit conversation.... but

felt that he could convince her

to replace her one intimacy.....

In his mind he liked this,

it showed alliance and integrity,

but this also made her more

challenging to him. he had to

win her ....

After all she was not turning him

down.........the wine was chilled

and plenty sweet.... the steak

deliciously well done and the

bullshit conversation surprisingly

intellectual in fact...it should

have been called verbal chess

or match point.....

He had maintained his confidence

in fact it had grown and he

was busting out all over..........

after all she had not turned

him down.... felt the time ripe

for turning to more sensuous

and intimate things...after all

she was not turning him down

39.   GO ON HOME WAY FROM HERE

Come here you tall dark handsome

black boy. What are you doing

around this neighborhood?..

Come just walking and looking,

or you come spying and prying

in us folks business?...

Sure enough think you lost

cause ain't been no tall long

dark handsome black boy in

these here parts for a long

time.

Hope I am wrong, but sure looks

every bit like you got your

wits about you. Now… you know

that could cause you a whole

heap pile of trouble round here.

Don't say much, do you?..

Guess, cat's got your tongue, buck

shot get it loose though...nice

and dandy it will.....

That's right go on, go on up

the road...that road taking

you a hard, long way from here

I know-ed you would go, when

I say 'bout that buck shot.

I did not mean nothing though

just want you on your way,

fore your father come home

and find his only ...tall....

dark.... handsome black boy

done found his way home.....

40. YES I SMILE, I DANCE, AND ACT SILLY WITH JOY

I keep aloft from you and all

of y'all ... for your comfort

lies in what you believe you

know of me and mine.

I smile so you can feel secure and

safe in your thoughts of me and mine.

I am here to make you laugh.

I am a good whatever you think

I am…that I am

If I don't smile you lose

your security and you become / are

full of fears of me and mine…

However… I reaffirm my security

and sanity of me and mine in

the knowledge of the thoughts

I have while I smile at you

and yours -- all of y'all.

Your destruction, demise, eradication

…and this makes me smile....

I look at you and see an ocean

wave after wave of atrocities

against me and mine… from you

and yours--all of y'all,

And I know it can't be long as it

has been and I smile, ...

I dance and I act silly with joy.

I try to keep aloft like the spook

that sat by the door...not to

disturb your reality, beliefs,

and security.

I am…that I am very happy

with my knowledge that your

awakening will be rude.......

41. WHEN WILL BLACKS GIVE THANKS FOR THE AWESOME BLESSINGS

When will blacks give thanks

for the blessing...

that they ain't war mongols

starting chaos all over the

world causing destruction

and division among all races

When will blacks give thanks

for the blessing…

that they ain't forcefully

exploiting...stepping on any and

all ...money at their helm

When will blacks gives thanks

for the blessing

they could ...give thanks

for the pretty brown skin not

prone to cancer, along with

that curly hair that helps

shield out those ultra violet

rays and heat of the sun as you

walk your homeland...breathe

deeply through those broad

nasals of that already warmed

air that blows over the homeland

When will blacks give thanks

for the blessing ...

they should.. give thanks for

pretty babies born more alert,

healthier and with greater motor

skills and greater chance of

long life.. Born with a heart of

love for all ...calm and passive

right brain personality.... creative,

yet living as one with the environment

When will blacks give thanks

For awesome the blessings.......

42. SEE ME AS BLACK

Yes see my color, don't insult me

by stating you don't see color,

Don't patronize me by saying you

don't see my color, don't insult me by

denying me my difference...

My people have never performed the

atrocities that your people have

piled on other races. No one

Black have ever killed, oppressed,

imprisoned, abused, misused, terrorized

castrated, raped, brutalized any other set of

people as you have...

Don't align me with your abuses on me,

Don't call me colorless.... since it is my color

that you used to justify the

indignities you piled on me,

Don't call me colorless, when my color

is why you have me homeless,

unemployed, hungry, uneducated,

drugged, and imprisoned—

Don't tell me you don't see my color...

when my color is what justifies

your hatred toward me,

Don't call me colorless, when it has

been your reason for sterilizing

my females, castrating my men,

labeling my children as retarded,

uneducated-able, bastards and monkeys,

You say you don't see color well

look at me and see me as Black

I am not the oppressor,

I am the oppressed,

I am not the slave master,

I am the slave,...

I am not the castrator,

I am the castrated,...

I am not the educator ,

I am the uneducated,

I am not the propagandarist,

I am the one that

propaganda addresses..

I am not the torturer...

I am the tortured,

I am not the pusher

I am the addict,

I am not the raper,...

I am the raped,

I am not the jailer,...

I am the prisoner

I'm not the capitalist,...the elite,...

I am the one she rides on...

You are a faggot and

I'm being fucked...

so see me as Black

For all you have done I am still

around looking up longer than

you can look down

See me as Black

because I refuse to lower myself

so you can look across....

See me as Black

and wallow in your in-humanities

toward me and mine

Because I don't want to eliminate

any of your shame when

Righteousness takes aim............

43. I HOPE YOU UNDERSTAND BROTHERMAN

Hey brother man / Hey cousin /

Hey blood / Hey grassroots

What's happening home /

How's it going man / Right on Bro

It's bad out here with

the man keeping us down,

with conditions being like they is…

Ain't no way out for the man

keep denying us our rights…

With all this prejudiced –

Klu -Klux-Klan and racisms

With these police shooting

us down for no reason … With

all this crime you ain't safe

nowhere – With welfare cutting

back and job quotas getting slimmer

Living is no slam dunk

Life is mean as a Mother blaster

out here and you know Bro

you my main man cause

you can understand …

You is grassroots – cousin –

Ace Boon Coon … you out here

You see it everyday

So I hope you can understand …

That if you got a dollar when

I need it – or I try to be an entrepreneur and

get your son strung out on drugs

and make him my runner

or drive by shot your little brother to become

accepted as part of my gang…

or Momma got her rent

money hid and I find out where it is

-     or your sister cashing her check

-     and I see it…

why I hope you can understand

I got to rip it off or kill you and her

trying – cause man - blood / love /

grassroots / cousin / brother /

it be's that way…

I got love for you …

try to understand brother man

        I hope you can understand … brother man

44.   OH MY LOVE PRAY FOR ME
AND WORRY NOT

Oh my love pray for me

each day, like you pray

for yourself...

And I will pray for you

each day, like I pray for

myself...

And we will be together

though apart as one....

To worry is to be with

fear and anxiety....

To care is to be with

love and faith....

Oh my love pray for me.

Let us care more and worry

less about each other.

Oh my love pray for me

and worry not....

45.   MELANCHOLY

I reach down deep to the inner
most parts of my heart, to find
out what is tearing me apart.
Need I suffer so desperately?
Can I free myself of such be-
wilderment rooted in the
phantoms of my heart, tunnels
of desperation, torrid pools
of torment that twist, turn
and toss me topsy -turvy...

As my externals smile, my
inners are racked with the
excruciating agony of
discomfiture...Fighting
with a heart that seems
to be in private arbitration
with the devil, as my outers
laugh... while feverishly
trying to suppress tyrannical
screeches created by the
atrocious, diabolical wrenching
of my heart.

You sit back

manipulating my heart as if

it were a marionette dancing

and spinning to the jealous

twitching of your aristocratic

thumb.

Is this sadistic ceremonial

rite a part of some scenario

to build my endurance or

a prerequisite to the taming

of the shrew...Then again,

would the credit of my

metamorphosis be fairly

placed on your shoulders

or would that just add to

your vanity...?

Nay, the honor is not yours

you may be the stimulator

but never the administrator

of such pandemonium....

Nay, I must look nearer to

find the crux of my melancholy.......

46. A MOTHER'S THOUGHTS ON UNFINISHED BUSINESS

Each living day, I live for the

next person. I pray for this one

and that one. I thank God for

this day and the one before

since I can't look to the next

day. Death hovers over me like

a UFO. Just waiting to get

me on target, for it to suck

the life out of me. But

I evade it, I run, I hide, too

many things I have yet to

do..

I must instill respect...

principles...and the love of

education in my children...

I cannot leave before my

loved ones are financially

stable and see their future

plans in the working... Each

day, each breath I get closer

to my goal ...nearer my death

and each day becomes more

precious....

Yet, my desperation

grows as my goals become

paranoia and I become

breathless, racing death

yet, full of life. Gasping each

little breathe, knowing it's not

worthy of being my last I

exhale with such force as

if inadvertently I have finally

resigned to death.

But wait, I tell

myself...are all in question

satisfied, have they become so

enthused with others, sufficient

in themselves caught up in

the lust of life so as not to

miss me...has life enwebbed them

like a spider, yet netting them in

such a way to catch them and

protect them from any of life's

perilous pit falls.

I pray for this

to be true but certainty escapes

me and another day approaches

as I wonder if my business here

on earth is finished......

47. THE SIMPLE LIFE

He wanted to know what I liked

He asked about football

He asked about tennis

He asked about television

He asked about sports cars

He asked about disco music

He asked about split dresses

He asked about rare steaks

...........baked potatoes

But for me he ain't said nothing

I like the simple things in life

champagne with almonds and apricots,

peanut butter and sliced apples,

liver pate with cheese crackers,

and imported beer......in an

atmosphere of place settings of

slim gold flatware and mineral

water in stem glasses.....

Yes...the simple things in life...

I like jazz and moody blues

in the evening...Bach and

Beethoven in the morning

along with chipped beef

on toast... chilled grapes

and tiger's milk, followed

by a mile and a half jog, a

row in the hay, nine hours

of good hard work, a warm

lavender bath and into

something extremely revealing

and start all over again.....

Yes I like the simple things

in life ....

48.   INSIGHT

Let us not ask when and where

but how and why we are here

for the how and why will tell

us the when ...where...and who

we are

The old man when asked why

he received no guest after

seven o'clock...stated for

they will turn around not

discouraged but with the

faith they will see me

tomorrow....

 For if they thought I would

not live until tomorrow

they would have come

yesterday.........

49.   This World Just Ain't What It Looks Like

Rich man out there saying he is poor

Blind man watching out for what he can see

Deaf man says hush I am listening

Poor man out shopping for everything

Dumb man trying to get a word in edgewise

Sanctified man sin in the name of the Lord

Old man praying to stay young

Young man stating he is too old

Intellectual man repeats the thoughts of others

Dreaming man's reality is fantasy

Walking man wants to be carried

Well man is a hypochondriac

Sick man refuse to take his medicine

Democrats voting republican

And the sinners testifying to the lord

No this world ain't what it looks like

The wise man asks.......

the blind to describe beauty

the deaf the sound of a melody

the poor what he would do with money

the crippled what it means to walk

the sick to experience wellness

the hungry to plan to a menu

the infertile to state wonders of motherhood

the lonely to explain the bonds of friendship

This world just ain't what it looks like

For the seer never looks within

The listener never hears the high notes

The rich cannot imagine being poor

The walker dreams of being chauffeured

The well thinks sickness is for the next man

The overfed cannot appreciate food

The mother learns to hate children

The friendly yearn for a moment alone

And the wise man forgets he knows not all

Some take life for granted

because death is for real....

While others say nothing is real

but our fantasies.... Most people

put things into proper perspectives

by seeing them through a blind man's

point of view...And thirst is meaningless

until the well runs dry....

This world just ain't what it looks like!!!!!!

50. EYES ON THE FUTURE, LET NO HURDLE BE DISARMING

Look back....

    to respect and cherish

the past

Look forward.....

    embrace life, love, imagination,

        fantasy and challenge with

           positive exhilaration, wonderment

           excitement and joy

Let no hurdle be disarming..........

Each moment a fabulous beginning

to a lifelong beckoning,

    climb and race to perfection

Perfection... the ultimate apex

reached only by those that live life

    with aggressive enthusiasm........

Let no hurdle be disarming......

As you live in present tense

with your eyes on the future

..........and the future a continuous

spontaneous generation and regeneration....

an extravagant evolution and metamorphosis........

Let no hurdle be disarming

keep your eyes on the future.......

51.   AND I THOUGHT OF YOU

Was it the autumn leaves

falling gently to the ground

The shimmering dew drops on

the grass

The orange sun setting slowly

on the horizon

The warm breeze blowing

my hair

The smell of seawater in

the air

The need to be held, to hold,

to talk, to listen, to be heard....

The need to be with you

to be two.... to become one,

to be alone, to be together

Was it all this or nothing

that turned my thoughts

to you.......

52.   STAY LONG MAN

I am looking for a stay long man

Stay long after the hugging is

over... after the smooth talk

is over, after the slick is

pass and you ain't trying to

get over... after there ain't

nobody else to impress and

you done seen every dress

on and off

A long staying man who will be

there when my hair ain't done

teeth are gone and all we

can eat is oatmeal

A long staying man when the

conning is over and the

conversation is fluent and what is

not said is understood as clearly

as the spoken word....

When the
ego stroking is over.... you

still have my back and I

have yours...when I laugh

at your jokes cause I know

you want to be funny and

you laugh at mine cause you

know I want to hear you

laugh not because it was funny

Long staying so that we can roll

over in the night and pat each

other to say I love you with

out waking up

Long staying so that when the

kids are grown you know I am

your baby and you are mine

Long staying when politics...

finance and race have separate

meanings

Long staying until seeing the divine
in all things shows us the true
beauty and meaning of life

I am looking for a stay long man
who knows life is what you make
it...not how many times you
can make out... Who knows it
ain't what you can get from one
another but what you can give
to each other....

A stay long man knowing that
it is not the staying when times
get rough but that times can't
get rough if we stay together

A long staying man with a life time
plan not a what we doing next
weekend

A stay long man who ain't jealous
of my friends and I ain't jealous
about yours

A stay long man who respects
what I am about and I respect
all he is about... not a yes man
'cause I ain't no yes woman

A stay long man that finds
me more important than the
newspaper and whom I find
more important than television

I am looking for a stay long man
who can handle a stay long woman
'cause I ain't looking for no
midstream changes

A stay long man that knows a
statement ain't an argument
and winning an argument ain't
making no statement for either
of us

I am looking for a stay long
man and he ain't easy to find...

cause I ain't looking to play

games....

I'm looking for a

stay long man whose looking

to live life with a stay long

woman he can call his ....

I am looking for a stay long man

I can call mine...mine...mine

53. HANDS HELD

Sometimes I just yearn to hold

your hand

hear the waves break on the rocks

thunder before the lightning

volcanoes erupt as stars twinkle

days melt into night

How life escapes ...if not for the

tender touches

as the snail crawls

the gazelle leaps with rocket speed

ecstasy unleashed, galaxies reached

...hands held...time stops...

54. ALWAYS THERE

She will always be with you

The beauty in your smile

The twinkle in your eye

The glow in the sunset

The warmth in the breeze

...sitting on the bow of the rainbow

....floating as the sparkles on the

incoming tide

She is there where you are

Where the joy of your life is

sadness pushes her away....

but it is not long before she returns

.....................as

The beauty of your smile

The twinkle in your eyes

The glow of the setting sun

The warmth of the evening breeze

.... riding on the rainbow

and floating on the waves

She is where you are...

55.   I TOUCHED SOMEONE…WHAT DID YOU DO WHILE YOU WERE HERE

I touched someone

and their world was changed

I touched someone

and became the light

They saw the world differently

They felt the warmth of love

I gave meaning where

there was question

They laughed with joy

They smiled from inside

They cried real tears

They experienced loss

and gave thanks for the gift

It is not how long you stay

It is what you do while you are here

I touched someone

I lived to be one hundred

I touched someone

gave their life increase,

substance and worth….

did the longevity increase / magnify

my value

No…my value was immeasurable

I touched someone

I lived two seconds …

never opened my eyes

I touched someone

gave their life increase…

a new side, new dimension,

new wealth

did the brevity diminish my value

No…my value was immeasurable

I touched someone and became the light

I touched someone and the world was

changed….

When asked what did I do while here

and why did I come…

I can state proudly…to touch someone

I touched someone and gave increase

and their world was changed….

56. A GIFT ON LOAN WE GIVE THANKS FOR THE PRIVILEGE, OPPORTUNITY, EXPERIENCE, AND GIFTS.

He was god's child and god lent

him to us

    We give thanks

And as all children that pass through us

they reflect us – how we live,

our strengths, our endeavors and

our adversities. He had many trials

and tribulations in his life…

He taught us self – discipline

    We give thanks

He exhibited great strength

beyond what we reckoned we could

handle…he showed courage

that makes us strong

    We give thanks

He overcame many obstacles that

challenged life …

He became independent…

he made us proud…

    We gave thanks

His smiles were our smiles

His tears were our tears

He lived life – its ups and down…

He was real

He gave meaning to our love

    We give thanks

He let no hurdle disarm him

he taught us perseverance

    We give thanks

It can be said that it is the

lessons we learn and teach each other

that completes our mission on earth

As he passed through us

we taught him….

As he passed through us

he taught us

    We give thanks

He has given us self – discipline,

      strength

  courage

     honesty

        faith

          pride

            perseverance and

confirmation of life and love....

For these gifts

     we give thanks

And as we give him back to God

in his death – an accumulation of his life's

experiences

he gives us life – an accumulation of our

experiences necessary for existence

     We give thanks

He was a gift to us

His value was immeasurable

His mission was accomplished

     We give thanks

57. PEOPLE - AN IMPORTANT ELEMENT

People like water, one of the most

important elements, on earth

besides air, go unnoticed, unappreciated

    drip – drop – drip

Many times people enter and exit

our lives similar to drops of water,

down the drain – a flowing stream –

a fleeting breeze, a rolling river

    drip – drop – drip

People like water move through

our individual existences without

their flow being felt, uninterrupted,

uncherished, untouched, unnoticed

    drip – drop – drip

The simple clean, crystalline,

transparency of water and people

does not decrease, minimize, take away

from nor limit the significant

importance of the elements …

equivalent to the chastity of

existence – virtuous, pure, invaluable

      drip – drop - drip

Let us spend this moment

acknowledging dripping drops of

water and appreciating

the passing flow of people

      drip – drop - drip

58.   THE BEAUTY OF NO PAIN – HAPPINESS

When the pain is so great

that you banish the feeling

to rebuke the pain / anguish /

fear / doubt / hurt / torment…

and when you cannot bear to feel

any more … numbness arrives

You reach for the pain

locate it – to stop it…

only to find you do not feel pain

…. no pain comes …. no hurt….

questionable happiness prevails

…endures – the beauty of no pain

the numbness that comes

When your pain is another persons

pleasure … its reality leads to

no pain - the beauty of no pain….

and the happiness that comes

with its knowledge of the death

of pain – the half cup –

the birth of happiness

The grave is dug

the cup runneth over and

the two dimensions become

one and the smile is engraved

……….tears no more

59.   A FRIEND FOR THE NIGHT

Sometimes you just need a friend for the night

Hold me tight and make the world feel right

Invade inner sanction – fireworks explore

volcanoes erupt – lightning strikes

reality is super-induced…the universe evolves

Hold me tight and make the world feel right

for sometimes you just need a friend for the night

Relinquish my rights to all your might

Surmount yielding to overwhelming fright

as we succumb to the feelings of emotional reeling

For sometimes you just need a friend for the night

hold me tight and make the world feel right

Surrender might – indulge for a night – lose control

as power takes hold – saturate the void

grasp the imaginary - annihilate the trepidation

vanquish the mundane - be spontaneously emancipated

never ever the same

Hold me tight with all your might

and make the world feel right

sometimes you just need a friend for the night

60. GRANNY WHEN YOU GON DIE

Oh girl no time soon … since

you do not die when you got

things to do

And I got five – six things to do

today. …already put off two

things …. meaning I got seven –

eight things to do tomorrow

…. and gon put off three – four

of them…. meaning I got nine – ten

things to do the day after….

God do not call you until you

finish the work he put you here

for …. So look like I'll be here

quite some time more, just

to finish the things I got

to do

… not counting the

things I want to do, need to do,

or try to improve on doing

plus the things I do for others

Oh baby girl granny ain't

going nowhere from here soon…

61.   THE LAST LAUGH OR A COMICAL TRAGEDY

It would be a comedy

if the tragedy was not so great,

that lives of perfection

should exhibit so much defection.

Is it the apex or the base that

deceives the balance or is it

the ideological balance that led

to its toppling –

        disintegration –

            erosion of

that which is baseless.

Too much caring – overindulgence

in caution or the aggressive

blocking of movement to and fro.

Lack of flow or an unnoticed

washout like an ebb tide…

like dawn to dusk…

like a short time prior to a long time

like a long time prior to a short

neither here or there

up nor down – spring nor fall

sweet nor bitter

      beginning nor end.

More likely the end of a great

beginning…with its center a

sobering plateau – a warm valley

whose detail free simplicity

centers its complexity

Those that laugh first and last

will cry longest as the joke

is recognized

      of this tragedy

           that is

smiled away as a comedy

Like one that makes…

a musical … a drama

an adventure … a satire

the customer … the salesman

the patient … the doctor

the victim … the perpetrator

the listener … the speaker

the dancer … the song

the treasure … the trash

the evening … the dawn

the prayer … the testimony

     of this comedy

         that allows us

to hear the tragedy of silence

and realize the beauty of

bringing light to the darkness

of the tragedy / comedy

     of too much said …

62.   YOU ARE PROMISED TOMORROW

You are promised tomorrow much

to the contrary of the famous

line 'you're not promised tomorrow'

I must inform you that you are.....

God never meant for you to arrive

here on a day-to-day basis. Life

has in all religions been seen as a

stay here on earth with death

causing you to spend time on the

next plane whether in heaven or

in hell.... reincarnation or spirit

world or purgatory with the whole

prerequisite for any of these

being solely based on how you

lived today...

So tomorrow is

a guarantee for reward, for

redemption, for punishment, for

repentance, for upgrading, for

immortality or just a rest before

your rebirth...

Made in the image
of the Most High we are here to
suffer nothing... Here only to have
and enjoy everything, here supplied
with all things worth living for...
Live life abundantly.

A life filled with inner riches of
love, happiness, health...Yes health
born in the lord's image you are
born perfect...free of flaws...

Yes
you are promised tomorrow filled
with inner peace and security
mixed with pride, confidence,
commonsense and a support system
of the millions that came before
you and the many more coming
after you......

63.   LIFE IS A HORSE RACE

Frustration is a horse that I ride in the race toward the finish line…

the Vertical crisscrosses the Horizontal in religious symbolism as

Life takes a turn toward Fanatical Favor … Dreams Dashed… Plans

Smashed …Wishes Unrealized… as the horses speed / trots / races to
the finish line – jockeying to first place in front of Goal-setter, Plan
Fitter, Hope-maker, Success / Prosperity, New Beginnings and Life
Culmination.

All racing Hiding yet showing Frustration with Determination to the
finish line with Long Suffering and Self -Sacrificing bringing up the rear.
keeping an eye on Celebration weaving in and out the crowd screaming
for Break -A –Leg, Shattered Dreams …Frustration got this race and
holding his place…don't let Reality check in…

there is always time to change horses with

more Beauty and Pride, Harmony and Love taking the high road. maybe
we should bet on Happy Horse and Gay Fashion…Super-size It flies pass
toward the now Finish line leaving Frustration in the dusk…

Life can kick butt if you ride that horse or forget the choice of change
during the race

Break Free and Loose and Set The Pace … during the race the chance of
your life …you make the decision to select to saddle up either Underdog
or Top-dog just don't let Frustration win.

64. SMELLING MY OWN COFFEE

Smelling my own coffee

Focusing on me

It is all about me …

The warm …The heat …The passion

The calm …The cool …The comfort

The strength …The depth

      The robustness of my coffee

Focusing on me …the inner me

break down the walls

shed the skin

loose the boundaries

      get to the core

There is only the strength

no weaknesses

There is only the future

no past

The now escapes before

we can get the word out

It is not about where I am

for life moves too fast …

I am already past being there

It is all about me as I

fumble …stumble …tumble

into my future

       The surreal is real

Drop the extraneous paraphernalia

It is not about the id

nor the ego

The smell of my own coffee

focuses on me

It is all about me

The energy, the aroma, the color,

The warmth, the clarity

The unmistakable uniqueness

       of the flavor of me

The smell of my own coffee …

Focusing on me …

Lets my light shine

Awakens me

Stimulates me

Invigorates me

      Motivates me

Celebrates me

increases me

reveals the … I am … of me

Yes …smelling my coffee

acknowledges the genuine me

and reveals the essence of my

mission and purpose …

65.   WHERE ARE YOU...WHERE AM I

I ask where are you... where am I

Where is the beauty...where is the wonderment

The love and joy of life without you...

There is the longing ...but no belonging

There is the quiet ...but no peace

There is the ease ...but it is not easy

There is heat ...but no warmth

There is food ...but no fulfillment

The sun sets ...but there is no settle down for the night

The stars like the sun shine without the twinkle

and brightness that differentiates day from night

sleep and wake becomes the same without the

highs and lows that come with an active heartbeat

The sadness ...the gladness

The open ...the close

The ups ...the downs

The ins ...the outs

The hot ...the cold

The wet ...the dry

The hunger of it all...

I ask where is the beauty…where is the love

The joy …the learning … the yearning

The integrity of life…

The norms are strange to me

The strangeness now norm

No pain …

Just a lack of feeling, wonderment, and belonging

Part of the whole yet separate from it all

Trust and faith and fear and doubt…

play games with my sanity

Discomfort sits where comfort sat

Where is the beauty

      Where are you …

         Where am I

GLOSSARY

Compassion – kindness, empathy, fellowship, a character trait that extends from the heart straight out with no strings attached combined with mercy gives life a rewarding meaning.

Courage – calm, cool, collected bravery in the face of obstacles, control of fear and confidence, it is the coming to the rescue, not the rescue, morally, valiantly and fearlessly.

Death – culmination of life's experiences can also be seen as the end of one stage, just prior to the beginning of another.

Dedication – faith with action, pledge of devotion, respect, honesty, and loyalty.

Faith – optimism, one's personal inner positive reality, that which needs no proof but relies on trust and allows us to bear the pain and joy of life.

Friendship – to have a friend is to be a friend loyally with affection, obligation, love, trust, positive criticism and reinforcement; the oneness that compliments each other with growth. the noblest thing a person can do is to be a friend with no strings attached.

Honesty – genuineness, moral excellence expressed via one's integrity, cornerstone of love and success and friendship.

Life – a combination of experiences necessary for existence.

Love – dedicated affection and devotion, respect, honesty and loyalty.

Loyalty – allegiance, patience, resourcefulness, constancy, devotion, and love are ingredients

within the pot of loyalty. the receiver of the pot feels friendship, security, comfort, and happiness.

Lust – believed need for affection, desire for indulgence.

Oppression – feelings felt by the abused from the abuser can be fitted to the north from the south Vietnamese, the children of Israel from the ruler of the Egypt, east Indians from the Pakistanis, the blacks from the whites, the weaker from the bully, the employee from the employer, the feelings of powerlessness from the purposed powerful, can be claimed by every sector of human beings even girls from the boys, even Catholics versus the Protestants, etc.

Perseverance – sticking to your guns, hanging in there, discipline fortified with undying faith creating endurance that generates a system of success.

Procrastination – root of failure, indecision, fear, doubt, stagnation, undermining oneself.

Responsibility – shouldering duties and obligation not viewed as burdens both big and small, it molds leaders and allows us to get along, mature and grow, a mix of self - discipline, accountability, dedication, reflection, and obedience.

Self-discipline – is what adversity blooms, it's the calm that proceeds / follows and prevents many a storm.

Work – tedious, strenuous, exhausting drudgery – ones success is linked to attitude when viewed as a sense of responsibility, self- discipline, or an exercise in perseverance it can become a labor of love and life, a positive investment in self, the expending of energy for positive accomplishment, a means to a specific end.

Index

These expressions (by moment number) within the Index will connect you to the "The 65 Moments of Thought